THE
OZONE HOLE

© Aladdin Books Ltd 2003

Designed and produced by
Aladdin Books Ltd
28 Percy Street
London W1T 2BZ

Revised and updated edition published in 2003
First published in Great Britain in 1993 by
Franklin Watts
96 Leonard Street
London EC2A 4XD

ISBN: 0 7496 4949 6

Design: David West Children's Book Design
Designer: Stephen Woosnam-Savage
Editors: Fiona Robertson
        Brian Hunter Smart
Picture research: Emma Krikler
                 Brian Hunter Smart
Illustrator: Mike Saunders

A catalogue record for this book is available
from the British Library.

Printed in UAE

Environmental Disasters

THE
OZONE HOLE

JANE WALKER

FRANKLIN WATTS
LONDON • SYDNEY

CONTENTS

Introduction
5

What is the ozone hole?
6

The ozone layer
9

A gas called ozone
10

The ozone disaster
12

Using CFCs
14

The danger
16

Disaster reports
18

The human cost
20

An ozone history
22

Ozone friendly
24

What can we do?
26

The future
28

Fact file
30

Glossary
31

Index
32

INTRODUCTION

Very high up above the Earth's surface, the fragile layer of ozone that is vital to life on Earth is being destroyed — a disaster caused by humans, that may have a potentially vast impact on our environment.

By releasing harmful chemicals into the atmosphere, we have caused this layer to become dangerously thin. An "ozone hole" has been monitored over the Antarctic for many years and now a hole above the Arctic has been discovered. The ozone-destroying chemicals that are already in the atmosphere will continue to damage the ozone layer for many years to come.

Measures are being taken to stop the production and use of these dangerous chemicals. But are these measures sufficient to restore the ozone layer?

WHAT IS THE OZONE HOLE?

The planet Earth is surrounded by layers of different gases. Together these gases make up the Earth's atmosphere. Within the upper layers of the atmosphere, between 10 and 50 kilometres above the Earth's surface, is a thin layer of a gas called ozone. This ozone layer acts as a kind of shield, protecting the Earth from the Sun's damaging rays.

In the spring of 1985, scientists from the British Antarctic Survey (BAS) were monitoring levels of ozone above the Antarctic. Measurements showed that ozone levels had dropped by between 40 and 50 per cent. When half or more of the ozone in the upper atmosphere has been destroyed, scientists talk of a "hole" in the ozone layer.

By October 1987, this so-called "ozone hole" over the Antarctic was almost the same size as the entire United States of America. Its depth was as high as the world's tallest mountain, Mount Everest.

The hole

News of the ozone hole was first made public in May 1985, in a scientific journal called *Nature*. The hole has reappeared every spring since 1985.

During the long, dark Antarctic winter, strong winds and extremely cold temperatures lead to the formation of thin clouds. Certain chemical reactions occur naturally on the surface of these clouds. When the Sun reappears in the spring and temperatures rise, these reactions lead to ozone destruction.

➤ **The false colour maps (right) compare the size of the ozone hole in September of each year from 1981 to 1999. The darker the colour the deeper the hole.**

The map (far right) shows the ozone hole over the Antarctic on 17 September 2001. This may be the start of a recovery but it is still too early to tell for sure.

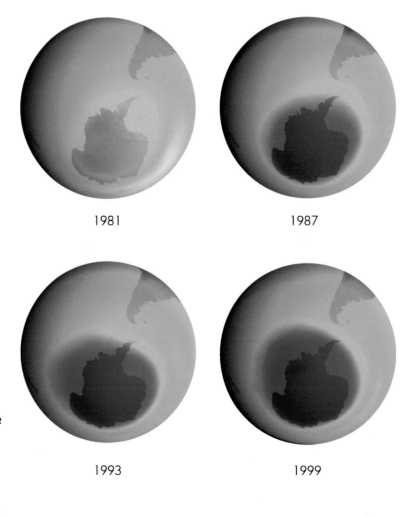

1981

1987

1993

1999

An Arctic hole?

Scientists measuring ozone levels above the Arctic noted that ozone depletion there had reached about 17% of its normal level in the winter of 1988-89.

However, the temperatures in the Arctic are higher than those in the Antarctic, and the special conditions that aid ozone destruction do not exist. A new study carried out between November 1999 to March 2000 found that a new hole in the Arctic is likely by 2020.

→ BAS scientists have been based at Halley Bay in Antarctica since 1957. They monitor ozone levels throughout the year.

In 1987, the BAS team was measuring ozone in the upper atmosphere using ground-based instruments. At the same time, American scientists monitored ozone from a flying laboratory (right) on board a converted DC-8 aeroplane.

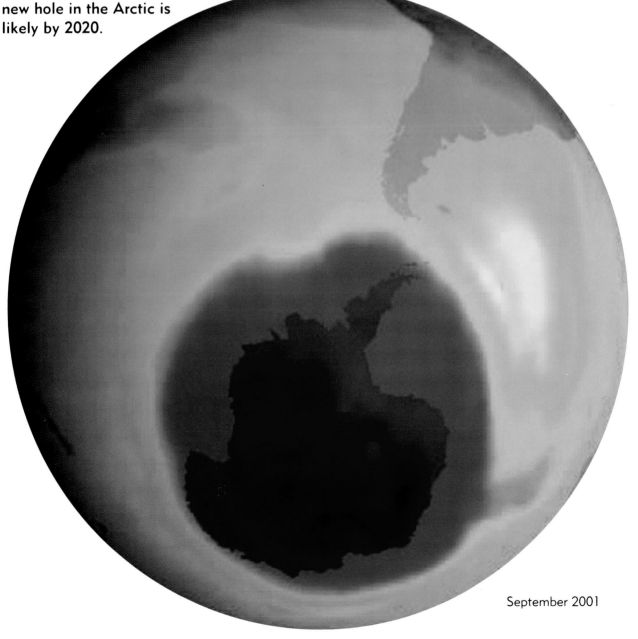

September 2001

← The 5,000 million-year old Sun is a huge ball of hot burning gases. The Sun is almost 150 million kilometres from Earth. Although the temperature on the Sun's surface is around 6,000°C, only a tiny amount of this heat reaches us on Earth.

Mesosphere

40

Stratosphere

10

Troposphere

Reflection
As the Sun's rays travel towards the Earth, more than 30% are reflected back into space.

Distance in kilometres

Troposphere
The troposphere is the lowest layer of the Earth's atmosphere. Within this layer is the oxygen we need to stay alive.

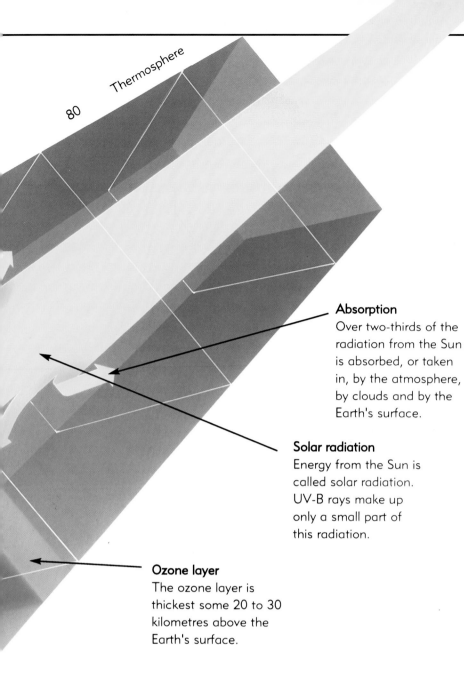

Absorption
Over two-thirds of the radiation from the Sun is absorbed, or taken in, by the atmosphere, by clouds and by the Earth's surface.

Solar radiation
Energy from the Sun is called solar radiation. UV-B rays make up only a small part of this radiation.

Ozone layer
The ozone layer is thickest some 20 to 30 kilometres above the Earth's surface.

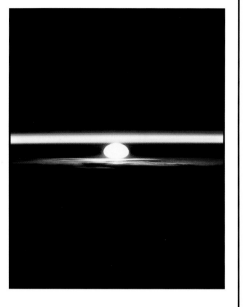

↑ Without the energy from the Sun, the Earth would be a cold, dark place with little if any life. This energy, called solar radiation, provides the heat and light that most living things on Earth need to survive.

← This diagram shows the different layers of the atmosphere. Beyond the thermosphere stretches the outer layer of the atmosphere, called the exosphere.

THE OZONE LAYER

Our atmosphere can be split into four layers: the troposphere, the stratosphere, the mesosphere and the thermosphere.

The troposphere reaches, on average, 11 kilometres above the Earth, but it thickens at the North and South Poles and is thinner over the Equator. The boundary between the troposphere and the stratosphere is called the tropopause.

The stratosphere extends from the tropopause to a distance of about 50 kilometres above sea-level. Within the stratosphere lies the ozone layer, which prevents the Sun's invisible but harmful rays from reaching us on Earth. These dangerous rays found in sunlight are called ultraviolet radiation (UV for short).

The more damaging rays are the ultraviolet-B (UV-B) rays, most of which are absorbed by the ozone layer. UV-C rays, the most damaging of all, have not got through the ozone layer, for now.

A GAS CALLED OZONE

Ozone is a form of oxygen, the gas that makes up almost 21 per cent of the air we breathe. When the Sun's rays strike the stratosphere, some of the oxygen within this layer is changed into ozone.

Ozone is a very unstable gas. It is continuously made and destroyed inside the Earth's atmosphere by chemical reactions and the action of sunlight. This process maintains a natural balance in the ozone layer.

The layer of ozone in the stratosphere is beneficial to life on Earth. But lower down in the troposphere, ozone gas is poisonous, or toxic. Ozone is formed in the troposphere when the nitrogen gas in sunlight mixes with hydrocarbons and nitrogen oxides. These substances are found in vehicle exhaust fumes and factory emissions. The result is a harmful pollutant which is called a photochemical smog.

Ozone

Every gas is made up of tiny invisible particles called atoms. The atoms are grouped together to form molecules.

One molecule of oxygen gas (O_2) contains two atoms of oxygen. Inside the stratosphere, ultraviolet radiation separates these two atoms. A free oxygen atom then joins up with an existing oxygen molecule to form ozone (O_3).

However, the newly formed ozone molecules can break apart very easily. Once again, single oxygen atoms are released. They join up with other atoms and molecules to form either oxygen or ozone. Harmful chemicals, such as chlorine and bromine, are present in the upper atmosphere. Their presence interferes with the natural balance that is maintained during this process of making and destroying ozone (*see page 13*).

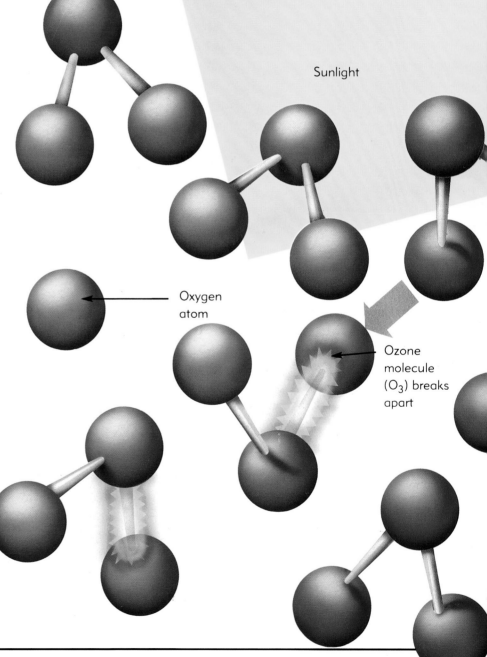

Sunlight

Oxygen atom

Ozone molecule (O_3) breaks apart

→ If human beings are exposed to the low-level ozone in the troposphere, their eyes, nose and throat can become irritated and their lungs damaged.

The problem of low-level ozone is most serious in cities that are surrounded by mountains, such as Athens, and in those where there are large numbers of cars and a hot climate, such as Los Angeles (shown right).

Ozone as a greenhouse gas

Ozone is one of the "greenhouse gases" which keep the Earth warm. They allow the Sun's rays to reach the Earth, and then trap this heat to prevent it escaping into space. The way in which these gases trap some of the Sun's outgoing radiation, and reflect it back onto the Earth's surface, is known as the "greenhouse effect".

Ozone accounts for 12% of the total amount of greenhouse gases (see right). An increase in the amount of greenhouse gases in the atmosphere may have caused the Earth to warm up by about 0.6°C in the last 100 years.

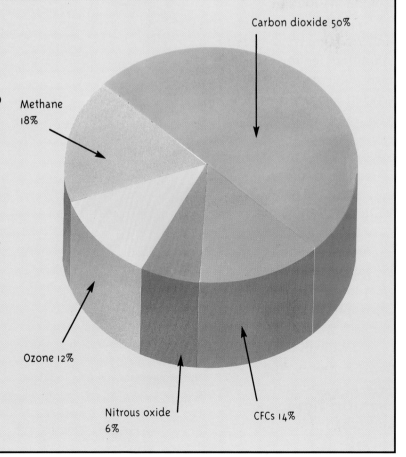

Carbon dioxide 50%

Methane 18%

Ozone 12%

Nitrous oxide 6%

CFCs 14%

THE OZONE DISASTER

Ozone levels vary at different times of the year, according to the amount and strength of the Sun's rays reaching the Earth. Scientists have now confirmed that an ozone loss of over 50% occurs over the Antarctic during each spring (September to early December).

The chief creators of this ozone loss are man-made chemicals, in particular chlorofluorocarbons (CFCs for short) and halons. Once they are released, CFCs rise up slowly into the stratosphere.

Here, they give off atoms of a chemical called chlorine. The chlorine attacks and breaks down the ozone layer without destroying itself. Halons contain a chemical called bromine, which attacks ozone in a similar way to chlorine.

Ozone loss may also result from non-CFC chemicals that contain chlorine, such as the cleaning fluid carbon tetrachloride. Another cause is the addition of huge quantities of ash and dust to the atmosphere after a volcanic eruption.

→ The Sun itself adds to ozone loss. Dark patches, called sunspots, form on the surface of the Sun. The appearance of these sunspots and other forms of solar activity (the yellow patches shown on the right) follows an 11-year cycle. Scientists believe that ozone levels are at their lowest every 11 years when the Sun is most active.

The largest solar flare on record was measured on Monday 2 April 2001. The big explosion hurled a coronal mass ejection (CME) into space, at a speed of 7.2 million km/h — but not directly at Earth. The largest group of sunspots was seen on 21 September 2000. The group was 12 times the size of Earth and this was only 2% of the visible surface of the Sun. The Sun gives off increased UV radiation during these periods.

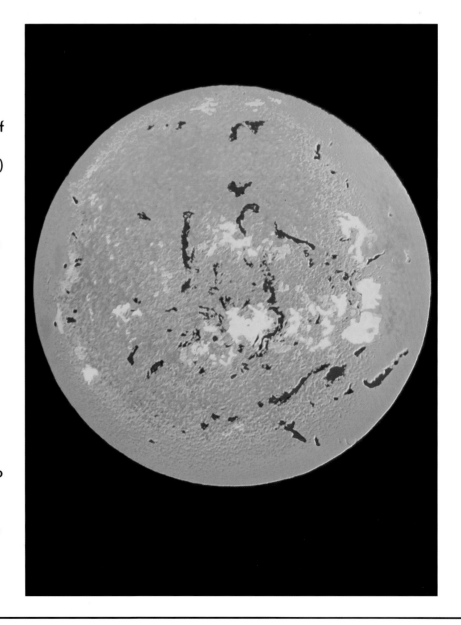

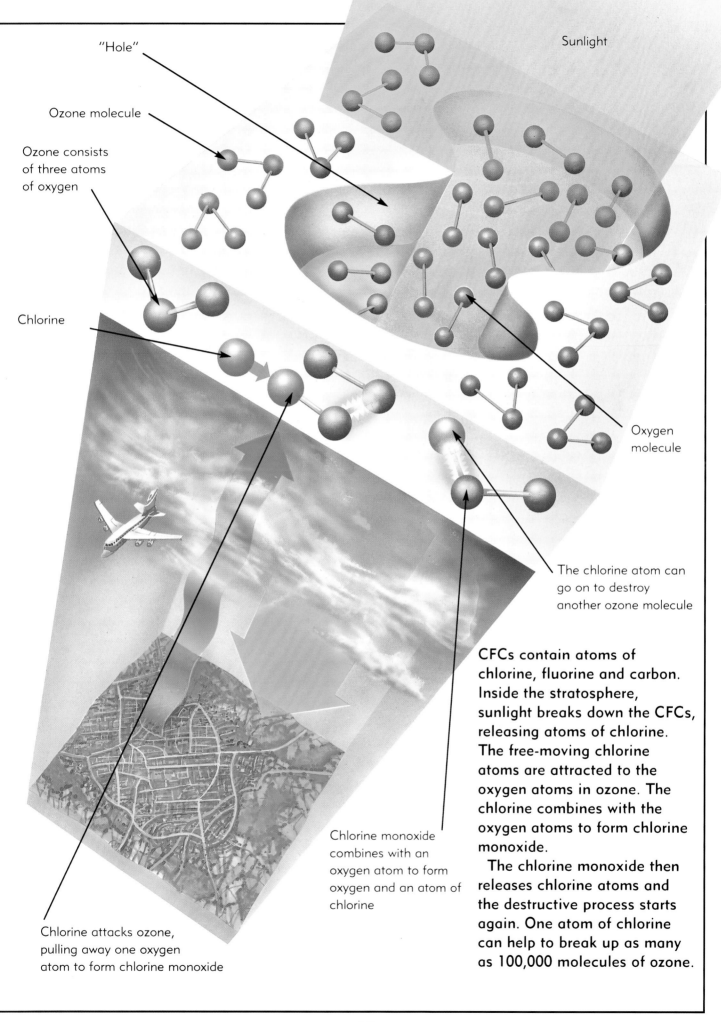

"Hole"

Ozone molecule

Ozone consists of three atoms of oxygen

Chlorine

Sunlight

Oxygen molecule

The chlorine atom can go on to destroy another ozone molecule

Chlorine monoxide combines with an oxygen atom to form oxygen and an atom of chlorine

Chlorine attacks ozone, pulling away one oxygen atom to form chlorine monoxide

CFCs contain atoms of chlorine, fluorine and carbon. Inside the stratosphere, sunlight breaks down the CFCs, releasing atoms of chlorine. The free-moving chlorine atoms are attracted to the oxygen atoms in ozone. The chlorine combines with the oxygen atoms to form chlorine monoxide.

The chlorine monoxide then releases chlorine atoms and the destructive process starts again. One atom of chlorine can help to break up as many as 100,000 molecules of ozone.

USING CFCs

In 1974, two scientists in the United States, Sherwood Rowland and Mario Molina, warned of the dangers of certain man-made chemicals. These chemicals, called chlorofluorocarbons (CFCs), could damage the ozone layer, causing it to become thinner. CFCs have now been identified as the single greatest threat to the Earth's fragile ozone layer.

The principal uses of CFCs are: as a cooling agent in refrigerators, freezers and air-conditioning units; to propel, or spray out, the liquid contained in aerosol spray cans; to manufacture, by a "blowing" process, certain kinds of plastic foam for packaging, for stuffing furniture and for insulation.

CFCs are very stable chemicals, which means that they do not easily disappear or break down into other substances. One of the commonest and most destructive CFCs — CFC-12 — remains unchanged in the atmosphere for over 130 years, and is responsible for around 45 per cent of global ozone loss.

CFC production

CFCs were first discovered in 1928. They were cheap to produce, did not smell or burn and they were easy to store. Their dangers were only revealed later.

CFCs are used as cleaning materials and solvents (liquids that dissolve or weaken other substances) in certain industrial processes, such as soldering and cleaning metals. In the electronics industry, CFCs clean microchips and other computer parts because they do not damage the plastic parts of the computer.

The pie charts shown right illustrate the different uses of two of the main CFCs — CFC-11 and CFC-12.

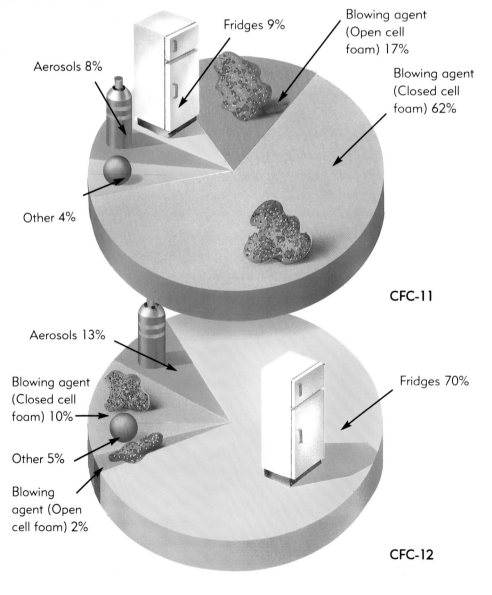

Fridges 9%

Blowing agent (Open cell foam) 17%

Blowing agent (Closed cell foam) 62%

Aerosols 8%

Other 4%

CFC-11

Aerosols 13%

Blowing agent (Closed cell foam) 10%

Other 5%

Blowing agent (Open cell foam) 2%

Fridges 70%

CFC-12

→The graph shows how the worldwide production of CFC-ll and CFC-12 changed between 1940 and 1990. In 2000, production of CFC-11 and CFC-12 stood at 9.9 and 24.6 thousand tonnes respectively. Although CFC production has fallen, the amount of chlorine added to the atmosphere each year is still rising. A number of other chemicals have an ozone-damaging effect similar to that of CFCs. These include carbon tetrachloride, which is found in dry-cleaning fluid, animal feedstuffs and pesticides; methyl chloroform, used in some adhesives; and methyl bromide, which is used as a pesticide for agricultural produce.

↓ CFC-12 is sealed inside refrigerators and freezers. When these appliances are no longer in use they must be carefully disposed of to prevent CFC leakage.

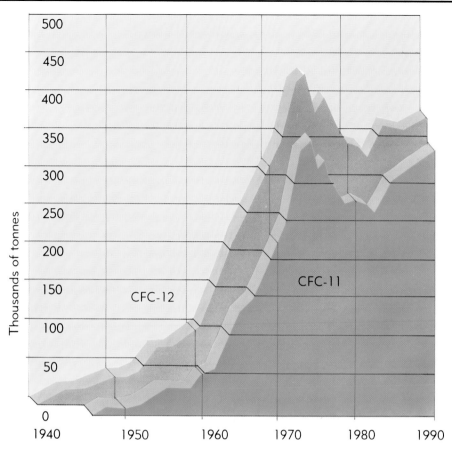

Year

↑ CFCs are also used in air conditioning units for offices, houses and cars (above).

THE DANGER

The ozone layer filters out much of the Sun's ultraviolet rays as they travel through space towards Earth. Only about 30% of UV-B rays reach the Earth's surface at the Equator, with around 10% reaching the Tropics and areas further away from the Equator.

As the ozone layer becomes thinner and thinner, increasing amounts of these UV rays are penetrating through to the Earth's surface. UV radiation is so powerful that it can cause serious damage to human beings, animals and plants. Exposure to UV-B rays can result in eye cataracts, which may cause blindness; in severe sunburn, and in the development of various skin cancers. Research has shown that even a one per cent reduction in ozone levels could result in an extra 50,000 new cataract cases each year.

UV-B rays may also affect the ability of the human body to fight off some infectious diseases and reduce the effectiveness of some vaccines.

Food chain

Microscopic plants, called phytoplankton, live near the sea surface. Tiny one-celled animals, called zooplankton, feed on the phytoplankton to form the first link in the world's marine food chain.

Within this chain, plankton are eaten by fish and other sea creatures such as squid. They are also eaten indirectly by larger fish and sea mammals, such as seals, which feed on the smaller plankton-eating fish. Even humans depend on plankton as the food supply of the fish they catch and eat.

UV-B rays can penetrate water to a depth of 18 metres, killing plankton in the upper layers. An increase in the UV radiation reaching the oceans and seas could lead to serious shortages in both maritime and human food supplies.

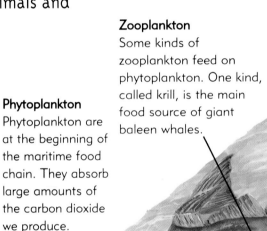

Phytoplankton
Phytoplankton are at the beginning of the maritime food chain. They absorb large amounts of the carbon dioxide we produce.

Zooplankton
Some kinds of zooplankton feed on phytoplankton. One kind, called krill, is the main food source of giant baleen whales.

Photosynthesis

In photosynthesis, green plants use energy from the Sun's rays to change water and carbon dioxide into carbohydrates. The plants use the carbohydrates as food.

Ultraviolet radiation slows down both plant photosynthesis and the development of new young plants. Increased UV-B radiation can reduce food crop yields.

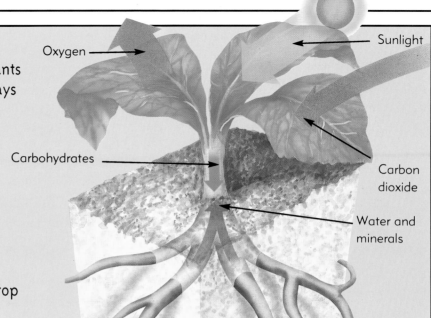

Oxygen

Sunlight

Carbohydrates

Carbon dioxide

Water and minerals

Fish

Fish eat the plankton and are then eaten by larger fish and other sea creatures, or caught for human consumption.

Humans

Humans are at the top of the food chain, removing around 100 million tonnes of fish from the sea each year.

↑ In the false-colour satellite picture of the Earth above, the red areas show where the greatest numbers of phytoplankton live.

DISASTER REPORTS

The 1987 Airborne Antarctic Ozone Experiment involved a series of flights across Antarctica to monitor ozone levels. The planes for this experiment were based in the world's most southerly city — Punta Arenas in Chile. In an area between 14 and 18 kilometres above the Earth's surface, ozone levels were depleted by an incredible 97%.

More cases of skin and eye disorders among the human population, and of animal disease and deformity, have been noted in the area than in previous years.

In 1993 scientists at the Climate Monitoring and Diagnostics Laboratory recorded the deepest ever ozone hole over the Antarctic. They observed that the ozone layer had been depleted by over 70%.

Since the 1980s, he ozone layer over Europe has reduced by 5% per decade and in 1999 was depleted by around 10%. Even if no more CFCs are added to the atmosphere, scientists predict that ozone levels will drop even further by the year 2010.

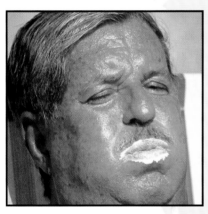

↑ **The US Environmental Protection Agency (EPA) has suggested that increased exposure to UV-B rays may cause 200,000 skin cancer deaths in the United States in the next 50 years.**

When the 1987 Antarctic ozone hole spread across to southern Australia, New Zealand and Tasmania, ozone levels over the city of Melbourne were reported to be 12% lower than usual.

Low-level ozone pollution causes an estimated $5 billion damage to US crops each year.

Skin cancer rates in Scotland trebled between 1979 and 1998. Increase largely blamed on short periods of intense exposure to the Sun.

April 2000
Environmental Protection Agency announces that ozone depletion over USA has measured between 5 and 10% since 1990.

Ozone levels in early spring over much of Europe decreased by 8%. In Switzerland, ozone levels have declined by 2.5% per decade (from 1973 to 2001).

March 1982
El Chichcón volcano in Mexico erupts, sending around 500 million tonnes of volcanic chemicals into the stratosphere.

October 1992
Ozone hole passes over the Falkland Islands in the South Atlantic and Tierra del Fuego at the tip of South America.

October 2001
The Antarctic ozone hole is about the same size as in the past three years, raising hopes that the hole is stabilising.

↑ Exposure to increased UV-B radiation can reduce the yield of crops such as soya beans, wheat, rice and peas. UV-B radiation can also destroy the nutritional value of these foods.

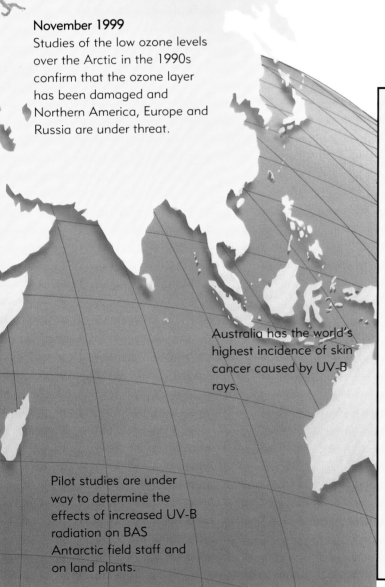

November 1999
Studies of the low ozone levels over the Arctic in the 1990s confirm that the ozone layer has been damaged and Northern America, Europe and Russia are under threat.

Australia has the world's highest incidence of skin cancer caused by UV-B rays.

Pilot studies are under way to determine the effects of increased UV-B radiation on BAS Antarctic field staff and on land plants.

A natural disaster

In June 1991, Mount Pinatubo in the Philippines erupted (below). Volcanoes add large amounts of ozone-eating chlorine to the atmosphere. Volcanic ash and dust also contain sulphur, which destroys ozone as well as absorbing the nitrogen gas that helps to prevent ozone destruction.

However, unlike CFCs, the volcanic dust and ash pose only a short-term threat to the ozone layer.

THE HUMAN COST

A decrease in ozone levels of just 1% could increase the amount of UV-B radiation reaching the Earth by 3%. This, in turn, would lead to an increase in skin cancers of between 2-4%, including the rare but often fatal type called malignant melanoma. This is just one of the frightening statistics about the dangers to human life from the ozone hole, and the increased UV-B radiation reaching us. Other statistics point to increased eye disorders like cataracts.

Skin cancers particularly affect fair-skinned, red-haired people who lack a chemical called melanin. It occurs naturally in the human body and causes skin to become suntanned when exposed to sunlight. Melanin helps to filter out the harmful UV-B rays that cause sunburn.

The world's highest incidence of skin cancer is in Australia. One out of every two Australians will develop skin cancer. More than 1.3 million Americans develop skin cancer every year, of which 50,000 die. These figures are bound to increase with depleted ozone cover.

↓ The malignant melanoma shown below is a highly dangerous form of skin cancer. Around 4 out of every 10 patients with this disease die within 5 years.

The occurrence of melanoma has been linked to people exposing their skin to short periods of very strong sunlight during sunbathing holidays.

➤ Doctors claim that children are particularly at risk if exposed to high doses of UV-B radiation during childhood. It is thought that between four and five periods of prolonged exposure to UV-B rays before the age of 16 years can increase the chances of developing skin cancer as an adult.

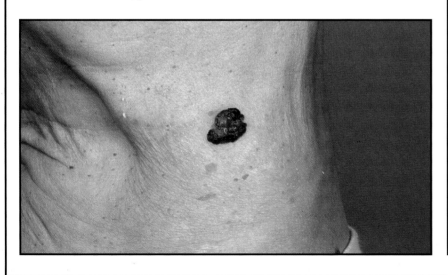

When the amount of UV-B radiation reaching the Earth's surface increases, the effects are particularly severe in urban areas.

In cities with heavily congested traffic, the levels of nitrogen oxides from car exhaust fumes are high. These substances react with sunlight to form harmful photochemical smog (see page 10). Driving restrictions have been introduced in Mexico City, in order to reduce vehicle exhaust emissions from the city's 3 million vehicles. The sign (inset) informs drivers of a traffic ban.

Dos and don'ts in the sunshine

DO
* Wear protective clothing and a hat with a wide brim
* Use a suncream with a high sun protection factor (SPF)
* Wear good-quality sunglasses that block out the UV radiation

DON'T
* Stay outdoors for long, without protective clothing, between 10 am and 3 pm
* Allow your skin to become sunburnt

AN OZONE HISTORY

In 2000, according to the US space agency NASA, the ozone layer over much of the northern hemisphere, including parts of North America, Russia and northern Europe, was depleted by up to 40 per cent. Here we look back at certain developments that have led to the ozone crisis.

1920s The first aerosol spray cans were used in Norway.

1950 Commercial production of first CFC-containing aerosol hairspray cans.

1970 Scientists express concern about danger to the ozone layer from supersonic aircraft.

1978 US government bans manufacture of CFCs for aerosol propellants. NASA launches Nimbus 7 weather satellite to monitor stratospheric ozone.

1985 Annual worldwide production of CFCs reaches 700,000 tonnes.

1989 Levels of chlorine monoxide over the Arctic are 50 times higher than expected.

1996 Both ozone holes are at 65% of norm.

2000 South Pole ozone hole covers 28.3 million square kilometres.

2002 Ozone hole over Antarctica splits in two and covers much of both southern oceans.

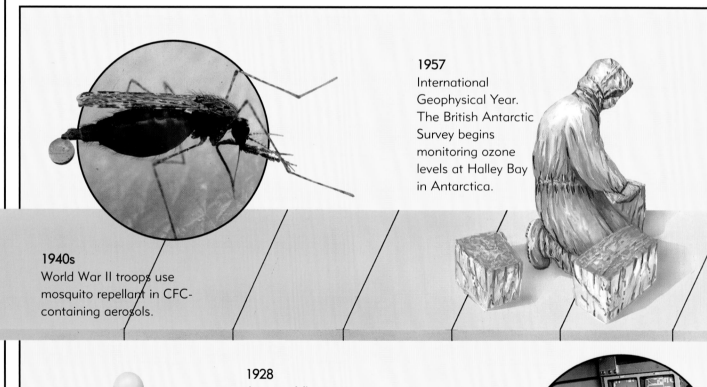

1957
International Geophysical Year. The British Antarctic Survey begins monitoring ozone levels at Halley Bay in Antarctica.

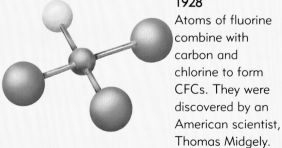

1940s
World War II troops use mosquito repellant in CFC-containing aerosols.

1928
Atoms of fluorine combine with carbon and chlorine to form CFCs. They were discovered by an American scientist, Thomas Midgely.

1974
US scientists warn of the link between CFCs and ozone depletion.

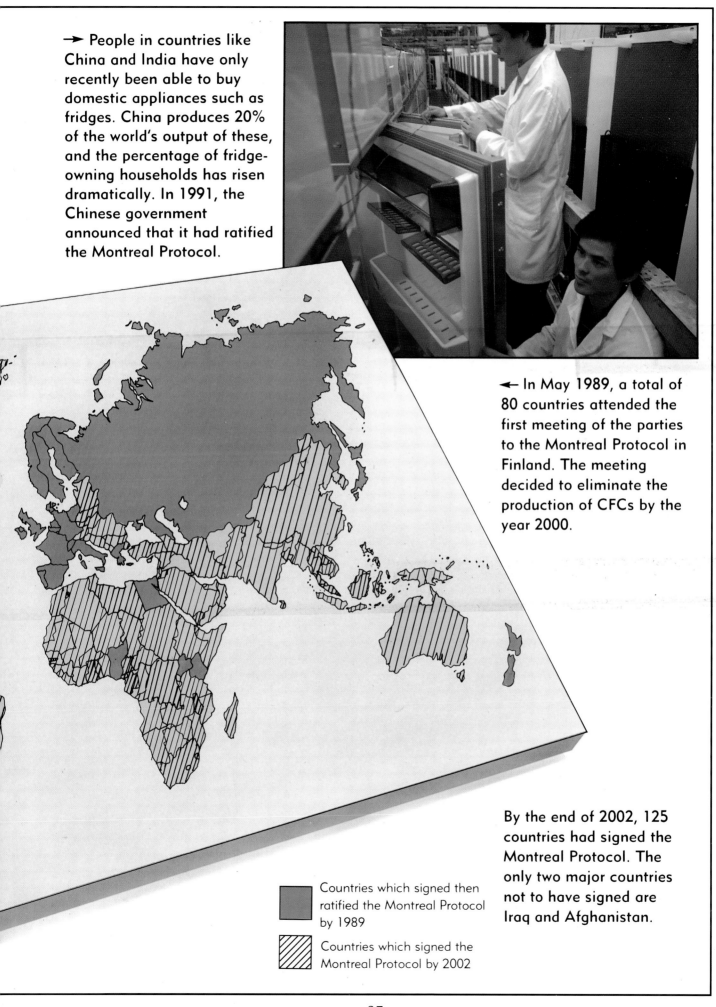

→ People in countries like China and India have only recently been able to buy domestic appliances such as fridges. China produces 20% of the world's output of these, and the percentage of fridge-owning households has risen dramatically. In 1991, the Chinese government announced that it had ratified the Montreal Protocol.

← In May 1989, a total of 80 countries attended the first meeting of the parties to the Montreal Protocol in Finland. The meeting decided to eliminate the production of CFCs by the year 2000.

By the end of 2002, 125 countries had signed the Montreal Protocol. The only two major countries not to have signed are Iraq and Afghanistan.

Countries which signed then ratified the Montreal Protocol by 1989

Countries which signed the Montreal Protocol by 2002

THE FUTURE

According to the World Meteorological Organisation, ozone levels in both hemispheres dropped by an average of three per cent per decade during the 1980s and 1990s. Some studies point to ozone depletion of between four and eight per cent in the northern hemisphere.

There have been some successes in the fight to protect the Earth's ozone layer. In February 1992, the United States and EC countries banned the use and production of most CFCs by the end of 1995, some 5 years ahead of the date agreed under the Montreal Protocol. In November 1992, the Protocol's timetable for banning CFCs was also altered to 1995. Other chemicals, like halons and methyl bromide were phased out in 1996, and HCFCs will be phased out in 2015. Sixteen of the world's leading chemical companies have joined forces to speed up the development of CFC alternatives.

However, throughout the world, governments must continue to kerb the use of CFCs and other ozone depleting chemicals. Due to the long life of these chemicals the damage will continue to be felt at the end of this century.

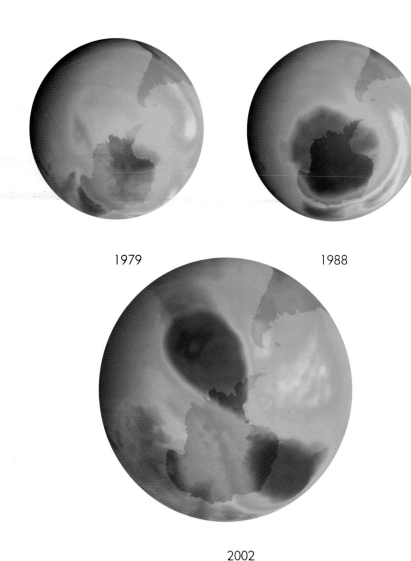

1979

1988

2002

← The ozone hole over the South Pole in September and October during the 1980s and 1990s was seen to increase. However, for the past three years the hole has been relatively stable. In September 2002 the hole was much smaller than previous years and was comparable to the size of the hole seen in 1988. The hole also split into two sections (see bottom left). Scientists have warned that this might not mean that the ozone hole has begun to stabilise or even heal, but it is more likely the effect of warmer atmospheric conditions.

→ At the 1992 Global Forum in Brazil representatives of indigenous peoples (shown right) and non-governmental organisations met to discuss environmental issues.

Many developing countries argue that the industrialised nations should accept responsibility for creating the ozone hole and should finance solutions to the problem.

The 2002 Conference discussed the possibility of providing additional finance to help developing countries to comply with the revised Montreal Protocol.

Laser

Operator

CFC destroyed

Destroying CFCs

Many proposals to combat ozone loss are still at the experimental stage, and involve the use of expensive and sophisticated equipment. One solution to the ozone crisis involves the use of laser beams (left) to destroy CFCs before they damage the ozone layer.

Another idea is to weaken the destructive effect of CFCs by pumping gases, such as propane and ethane, into the atmosphere. Yet another suggestion is to add extra supplies of ozone to the stratosphere, possibly using the unwanted ozone gas down in the troposphere.